S0-CNF-159

MIGHTY MORPHIN POWER RANGERS ™

TITANUS'S ™ BRAINTWISTERS AND MAZES ™

Written and Illustrated by Tony and Tony Tallarico
Cover Design by TXF Graphics

TM and © 1994 Saban Entertainment, Inc. & Saban International N.V. All Rights Reserved.
MIGHTY MORPHIN POWER RANGERS and all logos, character names and distinctive likenesses thereof are trademarks of Saban Entertainment, Inc. and Saban International N.V.

Copyright © 1994 Modern Publishing, a division of Unisystems, Inc. ® Honey Bear Books is a trademark owned by Honey Bear Productions, Inc., and is registered in the U.S. Patent and Trademark Office.

No part of this book may be reproduced or copied without written permission from the publisher. All Rights Reserved.

Modern Publishing
A Division of Unisystems, Inc.
New York, New York 10022
Printed in the U.S.A.

When they're not saving Earth, Jason and the other Power Rangers like to hang out at the Angel Grove Youth Center. Can you find 15 things that are wrong with this scene?

ita Repulsa has
layed a trick on the
ower Rangers! She's
idden all of their
elmets in this pile
f hats. Can you find
he Power Rangers'
elmets?

Take each letter through this maze to form the name of this town.

E G N R V A O G E L

The Power Rangers are lost in this old warehouse. Guide them out without running into Rita's Putty Patrol.

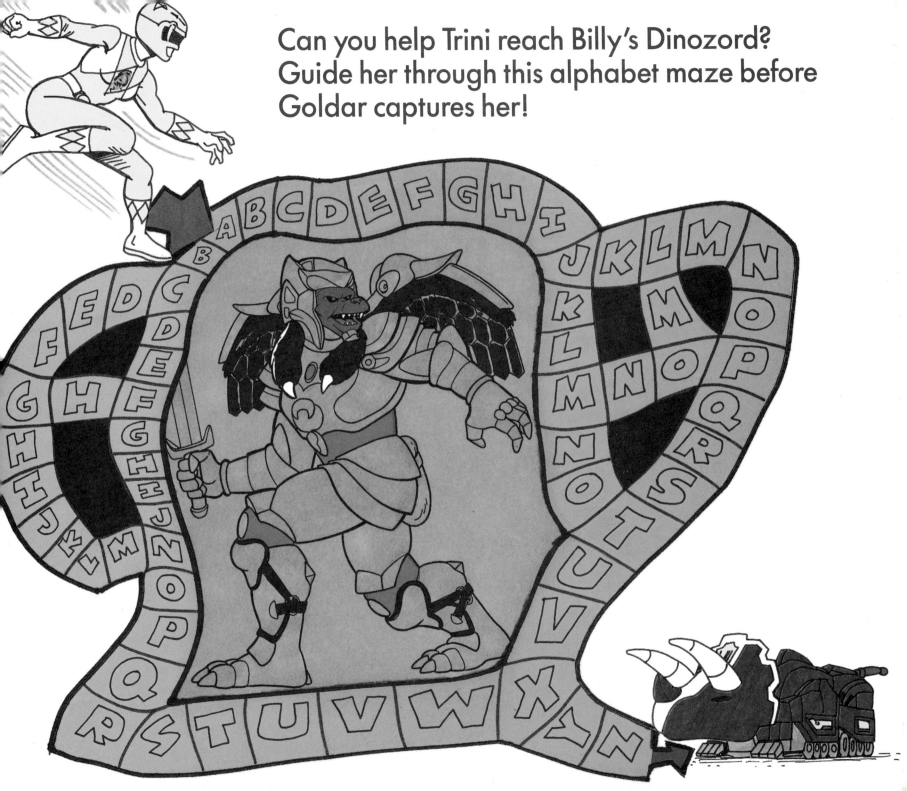

Can you help Trini reach Billy's Dinozord?
Guide her through this alphabet maze before
Goldar captures her!

Find the following items hidden in this battle scene.

APPLE BASEBALL CLOCK
DRUM KEY KITE
LIGHT BULB MOUSE PENCIL
SCISSORS SHOE
SHOVEL

CAN YOU FIND AND CIRCLE THE FOLLOWING NAMES AND COLORS IN THE DIAGRAM BELOW? THE WORDS MAY APPEAR HORIZONTALLY, VERTICALLY, DIAGONALLY OR BACKWARDS.

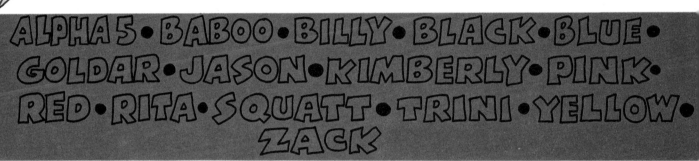

ALPHA 5 • BABOO • BILLY • BLACK • BLUE • GOLDAR • JASON • KIMBERLY • PINK • RED • RITA • SQUATT • TRINI • YELLOW • ZACK

Help Zack "morph" into the Black Ranger by guiding him through this maze.

Help the Power Rangers decode this urgent message. Use the chart that Jason has just called up on the computer screen.

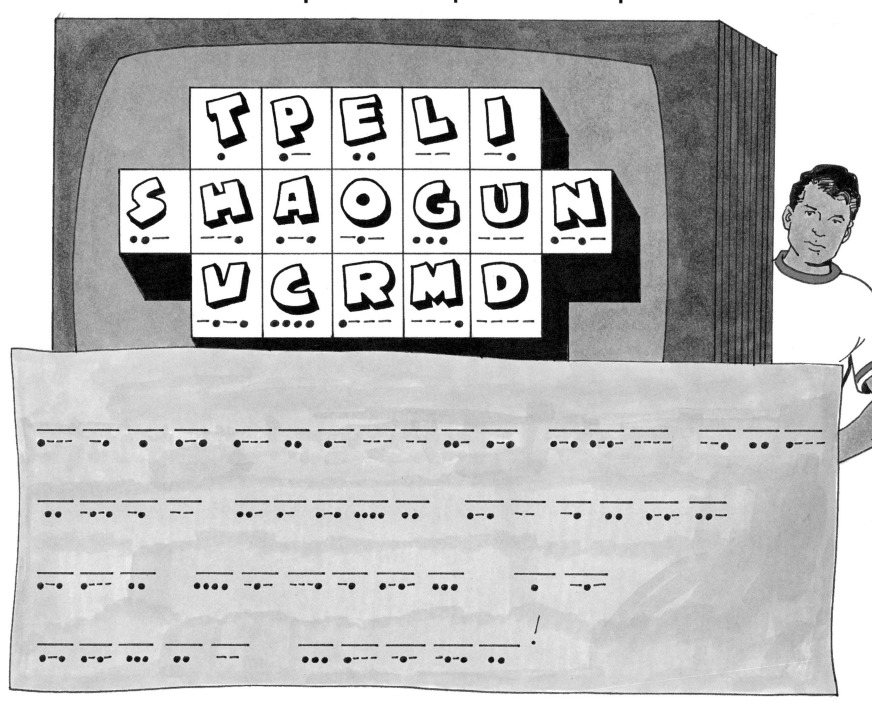

IF THERE IS ONE THING I DISLIKE MORE THAN CRIME, IT'S GOT TO BE **POLLUTION!** IF WE ALL PITCH IN, WE CAN KEEP OUR PLANET EARTH FREE OF POLLUTION!

Follow the correct spelling of the phrase POWER RANGERS DON'T POLLUTE to reach the clean air.

Guide Kimberly to Trini by choosing the correct path made up of letters in her name only (K–I–M–B–E–R–L–Y). Move horizontally or vertically only.

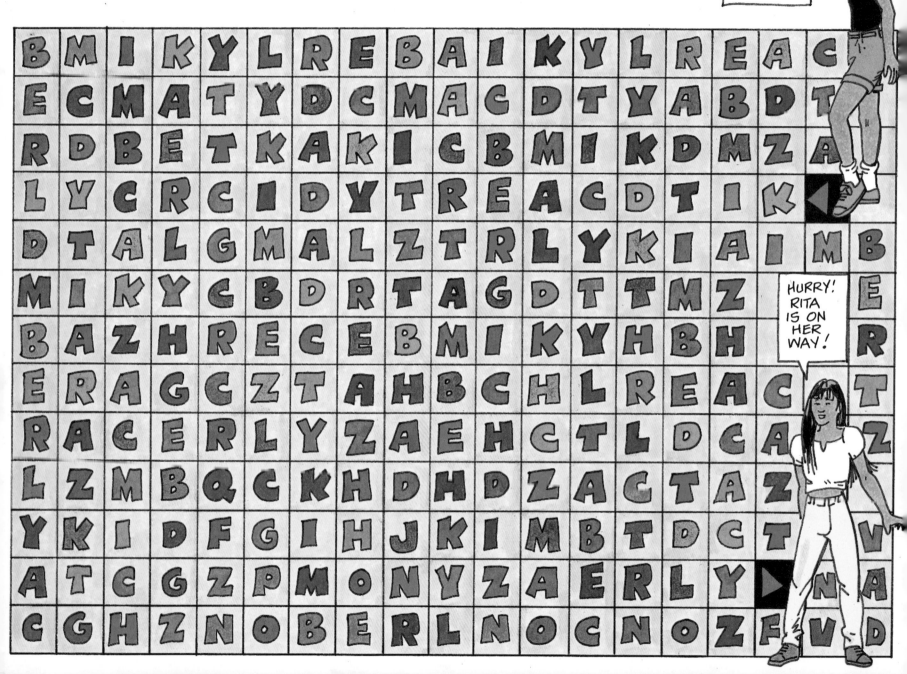

The Power Rangers have saved the Universe again! Now help them change back into teenagers by guiding them through this maze.

Help the Red Ranger fill in this wall before the Putty Patrol knocks it down! To complete the wall, use the letters in the top word to form the other words below it. (One letter is used twice in one word.)

Copy the lines from the top squares into the correct boxes in the grid below to form a special message.

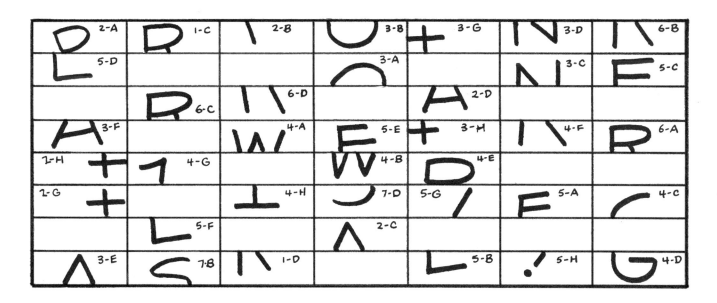

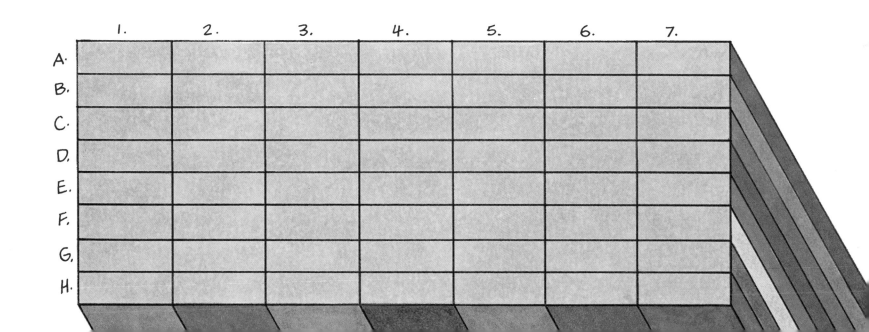

THIS LOOKS CONFUSING! CAN YOU FIND **16** THINGS THAT ARE DIFFERENT BETWEEN THESE TWO SCENES? KEEP IN MIND THAT ONE IS A MIRROR IMAGE.

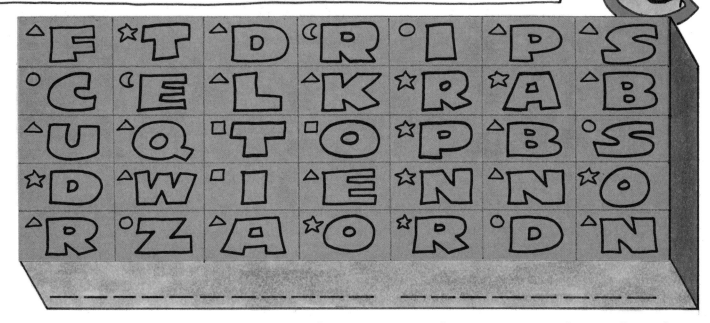

Decode this mystery name by using this special code chart.

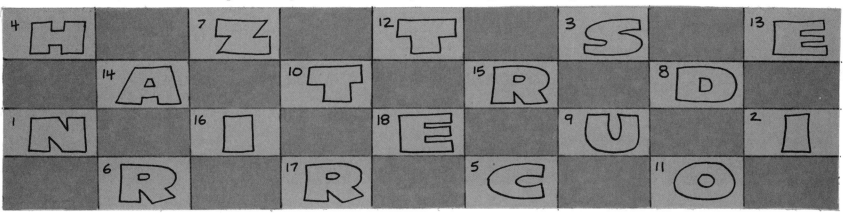

10 2 12 14 1 9 3 10 4 13 5 14 6 15 16 18 15 7 11 17 8

Solve this crossword puzzle.

ACROSS

3. _ _ _ _ _ 5
5. He's the Red Ranger
6. Evil sorceress _ _ _ _ Repulsa
9. The Mighty Morphin _ _ _ _ _ Rangers
10. Trini is the _ _ _ _ _ _ Ranger

DOWN

1. One of the Evil Space Aliens
2. He's the Black Ranger
4. Zack's Dinozord
7. Angel _ _ _ _ _
8. _ _ _ _ _ Grove Youth Center

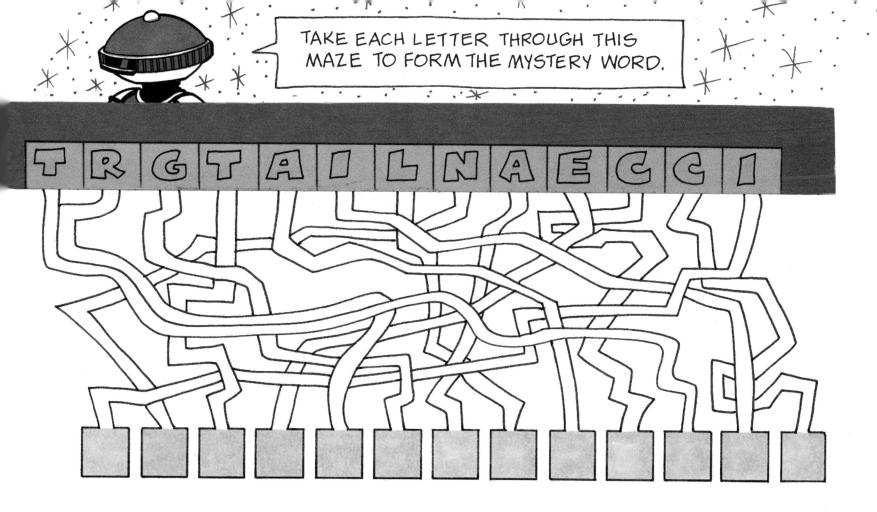

TAKE EACH LETTER THROUGH THIS MAZE TO FORM THE MYSTERY WORD.

T R G T A I L N A E C C I

Fill in the vertical columns of letters in the sequence of the alphabet to discover who gets his strength from the spirit of the ancient Tyrannosaurus.

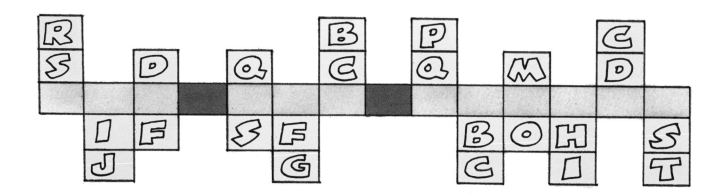

Guide the Black Ranger to his weapon by correctly spelling the phrase ZACK IS A BRAVE POWER RANGER.

To read this final message from Jason, Trini, Zack, Kimberly and Billy, fill in the blank spaces with the right vowels: A, E, I, O, or U.

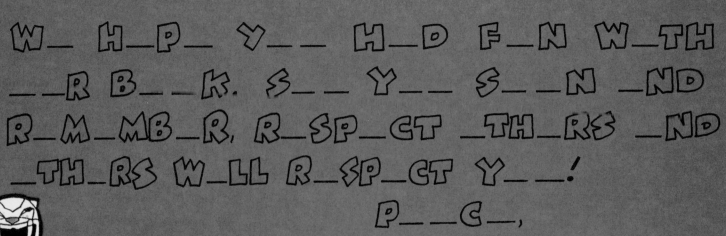

W_ H_P_ Y__ H_D F_N W_TH __R B__K. S__ Y__ S__N _ND R_M_MB_R, R_SP_CT _TH_RS _ND _TH_RS W_LL R_SP_CT Y__!

P__C_,
TH_ P_W_R R_NG_RS

When they're not saving Earth, Jason and the other Power Rangers like to hang out at the Angel Grove Youth Center. Can you find 15 things that are wrong with this scene?

Rita Repulsa has played a trick on the Power Rangers! She's hidden all of their helmets in this pile of hats. Can you find the Power Rangers' helmets?

Take each letter through this maze to form the name of this town.

SOLUTIONS

The Power Rangers are lost in this old warehouse. Guide them out without running into any of Rita's Putty Patrol!

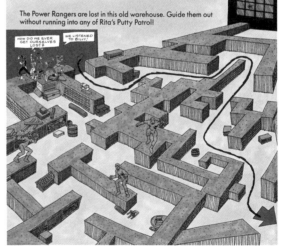

Can you help Trini reach Billy's Dinozord? Guide her through this alphabet maze before Goldar captures her!

CAN YOU FIND AND CIRCLE THE FOLLOWING NAMES AND COLORS IN THE DIAGRAM BELOW? THE WORDS MAY APPEAR HORIZONTALLY, VERTICALLY, DIAGONALLY OR BACKWARDS.

ALPHA 5 · BABOO · BILLY · BLACK · BLUE · GOLDAR · JASON · KIMBERLY · PINK · RED · RITA · SQUATT · TRINI · YELLOW · ZACK

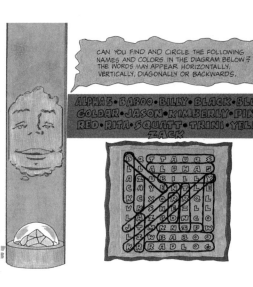

Help the Power Rangers decode this urgent message. Use the chart that Jason has just called up on the computer screen.

RITA REPULSA AND HER EVIL SPACE ALIENS ARE COMING TO ANGEL GROVE!

Find the following items hidden in this battle scene.

APPLE BASEBALL CLOCK
DRUM KEY KITE
LIGHT BULB MOUSE PENCIL
SCISSORS SHOE
SHOVEL

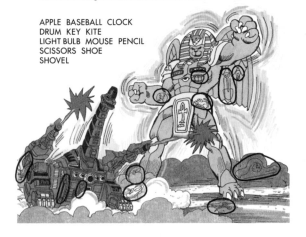

Help Zack "morph" into the Black Ranger by guiding him through this maze.

IF THERE IS ONE THING I DISLIKE MORE THAN CRIME, IT'S GOT TO BE *POLLUTION!* IF WE ALL PITCH IN, WE CAN KEEP OUR PLANET EARTH FREE OF POLLUTION!

Follow the correct spelling of the phrase POWER RANGERS DON'T POLLUTE to reach the clean air.

Guide Alpha 5 through this dangerous maze by choosing the correct path made up of ODD numbers only. Move horizontally or vertically only.

The Power Rangers have saved the Universe again! Now help them change back into teenagers by guiding them through this maze.

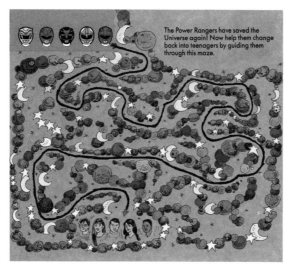

Copy the lines from the top squares into the correct boxes in the grid below to form a special message.

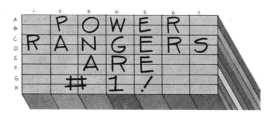

Guide Kimberly to Trini by choosing the correct path made up of letters in her name only (K–I–M–B–E–R–L–Y). Move horizontally or vertically only.

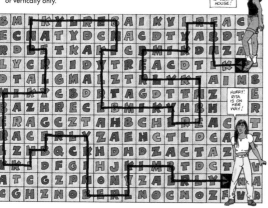

Help the Red Ranger fill in this wall before the Putty Patrol knocks it down! To complete the wall, use the letters in the top word to form the other words below it. (One letter is used twice in one word.)

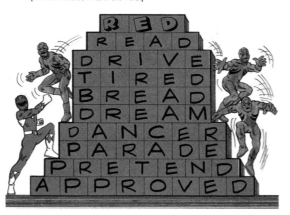

THIS LOOKS CONFUSING! CAN YOU FIND 16 THINGS THAT ARE DIFFERENT BETWEEN THESE TWO SCENES? KEEP IN MIND THAT ONE IS A MIRROR IMAGE.

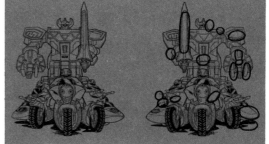

CROSS OUT ALL THE LETTERS THAT HAVE A TRIANGLE (△) IN FRONT OF THEM. WRITE THE REMAINING LETTERS IN THE ORDER THAT THEY APPEAR BELOW TO SPELL A MYSTERY NAME.

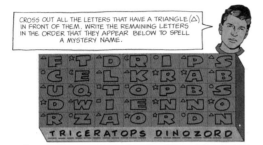

TRICERATOPS DINOZORD

Decode this mystery name by using this special code chart.

TITANUS THE CARRIER ZORD

TAKE EACH LETTER THROUGH THIS MAZE TO FORM THE MYSTERY WORD.

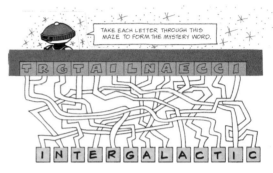

INTERGALACTIC

Fill in the vertical columns of letters in the sequence of the alphabet to discover who gets his strength from the spirit of the ancient Tyrannosaurus.

THE RED RANGER

Solve this crossword puzzle.

ACROSS
3. _ _ _ _ _ 5
5. He's the Red Ranger
6. Evil sorceress _ _ _ _ Repulsa
9. The Mighty Morphin _ _ _ _ _ Rangers
10. Trini is the _ _ _ _ _ _ Ranger

DOWN
1. One of the Evil Space Aliens
2. He's the Black Ranger
4. Zack's Dinozord
7. Angel _ _ _ _ _
8. _ _ _ _ _ Grove Youth Center

Guide the Black Ranger to his weapon by correctly spelling the phrase ZACK IS A BRAVE POWER RANGER.

To read this final message from Jason, Trini, Zack, Kimberly and Billy, fill in the blank spaces with the right vowels: A, E, I, O, or U.

WE HOPE YOU HAD FUN WITH OUR BOOK. SEE YOU SOON AND REMEMBER, RESPECT OTHERS AND OTHERS WILL RESPECT YOU!
PEACE.
THE POWER RANGERS